IMAGINE GOD

Rick Pribell

ISBN 978-1-64458-730-0 (paperback)
ISBN 978-1-64140-123-4 (hardcover)
ISBN 978-1-64140-124-1 (digital)

Christian Faith Publishing, Inc.
832 Park Avenue
Meadville, PA 16335
www.christianfaithpublishing.com

Printed in the United States of America

CONTENTS

Part 3

Part 4

PREFACE

The purpose of this book is to share a simple yet powerful revelation exposing how we can begin to know God. The potential is already inside of us. This can also be used as an effective workbook for introspective study. It may even serve as a useful guide on your journey toward salvation.

By understanding what it means to be made in the image of God, each and every one of us can then look within ourselves and begin to relate to God. This epiphany transcends our religious differences. It can transform anyone desiring to learn the personality of God, His likes and dislikes. This can lead us to appreciate Him confidently and form an everlasting relationship with Him, perhaps the way Abraham did before there was an organized Church.

My goal is for this revelation to become a branch of hope for you to grab, to pull yourself up by, and with the Holy Spirit begin climbing as you start to develop a real and more personal relationship with God. As you progress upward through the examples ahead to *Imagine God*, my prayer is that you *find yourself* closer to Him.

The benefit to you by completing the entire journey can be an everlasting peace that comes with salvation. This peace is built on the resolute awareness of God's presence and acceptance; an everlasting peace that "surpasses all understanding" (Philippians 4:7).

The order of discussion will begin with an explanation of how God made us with the ability to learn His character intimately. Next, we will review various examples that bring this to light and reinforce its truth. Then, we will discuss how to secure an eternal relationship with God based on biblical teaching. Finally, I share my personal testimony, and a commentary of my account regarding the image photographed on the front cover.

ACKNOWLEDGMENTS

Thank you, Lord, for my salvation. Thank you for using me as a vessel to share with others just how easy it is to get to know You as we think about ourselves being created in Your image.

Thank you to my family for all of your encouragement. Joyce, you are a true Proverbs 31 wife. To our wonderful children, Johanna and Joshuah, you are both living proof that dreams do come true.

Thank you to Reverend Andrew Sherman for spending invaluable time with me in Bible study. Thank you also to my supportive associates, neighbors, family and friends, especially Wendy Mahle, Philip Hall, Jina Levine, and Betsy Hawkins. And, thank you to Christian Faith Publishing for exceeding my expectations. Each of your special contributions resonate in this book.

INTRODUCTION

Discovering God's nature can be found within ourselves because we are made in His likeness. However, it is important to acknowledge that our true intended nature has been affected by sin ever since the fall of Adam and Eve from the Garden of Eden. It is also important to acknowledge that our existence is newborn, relative to God's infinite existence. Consequently, just like a toddler must learn to walk before he can run, so too our ability to know God is limited and will develop over time.

Our reaction to certain events, for example, may initially be clouded by prideful emotion and eventually evolve through grace, into Christlike, spiritually mature clarity. This is especially true when it comes to the subject of forgiveness, which we will discuss later. As we take this journey, we will also compare our perspective against Scripture in order to validate God's message from within.

PART 1

PROLOGUE

"God created man in His own image,
in the image of God He created him;
male and female He created them."
Genesis 1:27 NASB

Why is it significant that God created us "in His own image", so important that it is reiterated in this verse? It means that He has blessed us with the ability to know Him. *Like a reflection in the mirror of our soul,* by our own feelings and experiences, our own likes and dislikes, we can *Imagine God*—we are made in His image.

Evidence of this being true is the fact that positive stimuli produce good feelings in all of us. Conversely, negative stimuli cause us to experience bad feelings. This is because we are *all* made in His image. Therefore, we are *all* able to *Imagine God* and His perspective on what is good and what is bad, His likes and dislikes.

In the following pages we will examine our feelings, derived from some common experiences, in an effort to relate to God. Each example will be supported by relevant scripture so that we may get to know Him more confidently.

PART 2

OBEY GOD'S COMMANDMENTS

Have you ever had an experience when someone you knew stole from you or cheated you? How did that make you feel? Disappointed? Betrayed? By reflecting on those negative feelings, we can *Imagine God* rejects unlawful behavior and understand why He commands us not to steal.

A personal example occurred shortly after I began writing this book. I hired a handyman who struggled with substance abuse. To my dismay he completed only a portion of the job, and what he did finish was poorly performed. I later learned that he also stole from me and pawned some of my belongings to support his addiction.

Why did he do this to me? How could I ever trust him again? While I felt victimized, I used this experience to identify with God by how it feels when someone violates His commandments, and through His Word.

Eighth commandment, *"You shall not steal."* Matthew 7:12, NIV: *"So in everything, do to others what you would have them do to you, for this sums up the Law and the Prophets."* John 14:15, NLT: *"If you love me, obey my commandments."* John 8:34, NIV: *"Jesus replied, 'Very truly I tell you, everyone who sins is a slave to sin.'"* Luke 16:10, NIV: *"Whoever can be trusted with very little can also be trusted with much, and whoever is dishonest with very little will also be dishonest with much."*

REMAIN FAITHFUL TO GOD

God wants us to be faithful. What does it mean to be faithful to God? Consider the sanctity of marriage when two people are to love, honor, and comfort each other.

Now, what happens if one spouse learns the other is having an affair? How awful would that feel? Similarly, we can *Imagine God* is adamant about His covenants. In the same spirit that He commands us to maintain fidelity with our spouse, He demands us to remain faithful to Him.

Remember, God wants us to love Him, so let's not practice idolatry by worshiping riches, fame, power, or anything else above Him.

First Commandment, *"You shall have no other gods before me."* Seventh Commandment, *"You shall not commit adultery."* Hebrews 13:4, NIV: *"Marriage should be honored by all, and the marriage bed kept pure, for God will judge the adulterer and all the sexually immoral."* Joshua 22:5, NLT: *"But be very careful to obey all the commands and the instructions that Moses gave to you. Love the LORD your God, walk in all his ways, obey his commands, hold firmly to him, and serve him with all your heart and all your soul."* Ezekiel 23:49, NIV: *"You will suffer the penalty for your lewdness and bear the consequences of your sins of idolatry. Then you will know that I am the Sovereign LORD."* 1 Samuel 12:24, NIV: *"But be sure to fear the LORD and serve him faithfully with all your heart; consider what great things he has done for you."*

PRAISE GOD

Now let's examine an experience that will make you feel wonderful and consider how God would welcome it: one day you arrive late to work and your colleagues are unaware of your presence. You then overhear them in the next room, and they are talking about you. Suddenly your interest is piqued; how do they really feel about you? Then you hear, "I can't wait till he comes in. I am so happy that he works here. By the way, did you see how well he handled that problem yesterday?" They are praising you!

How does it feel to be valued and praised? Good, right? Through these positive feelings, we can *Imagine God* and how pleasing it is when we value and praise Him. Can you relate to this in your life? Now ask yourself, what is God overhearing?

Leviticus 26:12, NIV: *"I will walk among you and be your God, and you will be my people."* Psalm 150:6, NIV: *"Let everything that has breath praise the LORD. Praise the LORD."* Psalm 69:30–31, NLT: *"Then I will praise God's name with singing, and I will honor him with thanksgiving. For this will please the LORD more than sacrificing cattle, more than presenting a bull with its horns and hooves."*

PRIORITIZE GOD

Reflect back to when you participated in some kind of competition. Do you remember the anxiety you experienced? From early on, haven't we learned that it feels good to win, to be number one? And doesn't it feel demoralizing to lose, especially to finish last?

Nobody wants to be disregarded and feel irrelevant. Maybe we were made this way so we can *Imagine God* desires to be relevant in our lives and does not want to be disregarded either.

In the same way that we value winning, God values winning our affection and wants us to strive and win His favor. So, let's make Him our first priority.

1 Corinthians 9:23–24, NASB: *"I do all things for the sake of the gospel, so that I may become a fellow partaker of it. Do you not know that those who run in a race all run, but only one receives the prize? Run in such a way that you may win."* Exodus 20:3, NASB: *"You shall have no other gods before Me."* Deuteronomy 5:7, NIV: *"You shall have no other gods before me."* Matthew 22:37–39, NIV: *"Jesus replied: 'Love the Lord your God with all your heart and with all your soul and with all your mind.' This is the first and greatest commandment. And the second is like it: 'Love your neighbor as yourself.'"*

PERFORM FOR GOD

When we disregard God in our lives, sin will take over. From the previous example, we can relate our desire for winning to God's desire to be first in our lives and for us to make Him our priority.

Unfortunately, instead of serving God, many of us become vain, consumed with competition and winning for carnal pleasure—from competitive sports to beauty pageants to politics to making money. Sadly, many people mistakenly measure their own worth by comparing themselves to others or by how other people judge their performances.

Fortunately, in the same way that we will give helpful and honest advice to those who seek our counsel, we can *Imagine God* is loving and full of empathy, concerning our shortsightedness; He even informs us about these misunderstandings in the following scripture.

Philippians 2:3, NIV: *"Do nothing out of selfish ambition or vain conceit. Rather, in humility value others above yourselves."* 2 Corinthians 10:12, NASB: *"For we are not bold to class or compare ourselves with some of those who commend themselves; but when they measure themselves by themselves and compare themselves with themselves, they are without understanding."* 1 Corinthians 9:25, NLT: *"All athletes are disciplined in their training. They do it to win a prize that will fade away, but we do it for an eternal prize."* Luke 16:15, NLT: *"Then he said to them, 'You like to appear righteous in public, but God knows your hearts. What this world honors is detestable in the sight of God.'"*

WORSHIP GOD

Have you ever truly wanted the affection of another? And, if you were fortunate to get it, didn't that make you feel wonderful? However, if you did not win their affection, and it went to someone else, how did that make you feel? Jealous?

Perhaps we were made to feel that way in order to *Imagine God* is a jealous God. After all, while He allows us to make our own choices, God made us for His glory; He has given us everything we have, and He desires for us to choose a loving relationship with Him.

Exodus 34:14, NIV: *"Do not worship any other god, for the LORD, whose name is Jealous, is a jealous God."* Romans 11:36, NLT: *"For everything comes from him and exists by his power and is intended for his glory. All glory to him forever! Amen."* Exodus 20:2–6, NASB, *"I am the LORD your God, who brought you out of the land of Egypt, out of the house of slavery. You shall have no other gods before Me. You shall not make for yourself an idol, or any likeness of what is in heaven above or on the earth beneath or in the water under the earth. You shall not worship them or serve them; for I, the LORD your God, am a jealous God, visiting the iniquity of the fathers on the children, on the third and the fourth generations of those who hate Me, but showing lovingkindness to thousands, to those who love Me and keep My commandments."*

WELCOME GOD'S GUIDANCE

Family is another one of God's gifts through which we can imagine Him. To protect children, it is with great care that we foresee the future to ensure their safety. We childproof our homes before they even learn to crawl.

When our children learn to walk, we teach them not to get close to a hot stove and explain the danger of getting burned. As they grow older, and disobey by running through the kitchen when hot food is being prepared after knowing the risks, they may need discipline.

We must continue to watch over and guide them. So too we can *Imagine God* working in our lives to keep us safe, teach, and guide us. We all have an independent nature and want to do what *we* want, sometimes disregarding the peril. As with our own children, our Heavenly Father can foresee the result of our actions and may rebuke us out of love.

Deuteronomy 8:5, NIV: *"Know then in your heart that as a man disciplines his son, so the LORD your God disciplines you."* Hebrews 12:5–6, NIV: *"Do not make light of the Lord's discipline, and do not lose heart when he rebukes you, because the Lord disciplines the one he loves, and he chastens everyone he accepts as his son."*

EMULATE GOD'S CHARACTER

Another interesting fact is how children reflect the image of their parents, often physically by their shared appearances, and otherwise. Children even assume the characteristics of their parents through similar values, attributes, and desires.

Perhaps God designed us this way for us to recognize that we are all made in the image of our father and mother and, by extension, our heavenly Father above.

As our children learn to mimic our earthly characteristics, we can *Imagine God* wanting us to take on His character and imitate Christ in everything we do.

Genesis 5:3, NIV: *"When Adam had lived 130 years, he had a son in his own likeness, in his own image; and he named him Seth."* 1 John 2:6, NLT: *"Those who say they live in God should live their lives as Jesus did."* 1 Corinthians 11:1, NASB: *"Be imitators of me, just as I also am of Christ."*

SUBMIT TO GOD'S AUTHORITY

In a traditional family, the head of the household, along with his helpmate, will naturally make the family decisions: with whom to associate, what expectations to establish, when to give, where to live.

On a much larger scale, we can *Imagine God* is the decision maker and sovereign ruler over His kingdom and, in the end, like always, it is His will that reigns.

1 Timothy 3:4–5, NLT: *"He must manage his own family well, having children who respect and obey him. For if a man cannot manage his own household, how can he take care of God's church?"* Psalm 46:10, NIV: *"He says 'Be still, and know that I am God; I will be exalted among the nations, I will be exalted in the earth.'"* Psalm 103:19, NIV: *"The LORD has established his throne in heaven, and his kingdom rules over all."* Psalm 115:3, NIV: *"Our God is in heaven; he does whatever pleases him."* Matthew 6:10, NIV: *"Your kingdom come, your will be done, on earth as it is in heaven"*.

HONOR GOD

As parents, we have experienced the effects of our children's behavior. For example, we understand how disappointing and embarrassing it feels when we instruct our children and they respond with rebellion.

Surely we can *Imagine God* feeling disappointment when we, His children, do not obey Him. And we can certainly understand why He commands us to honor our earthly father and mother; the same way He wants us to honor Him, our heavenly Father.

Fifth Commandment, *"Honor your father and mother."* Deuteronomy 5:16, NIV: *"Honor your father and your mother, as the LORD your God has commanded you, so that you may live long and that it may go well with you in the land the LORD your God is giving you."* 1 Timothy 1:17, NLT: *"All honor and glory to God forever and ever! He is the eternal King, the unseen one who never dies; he alone is God, Amen."*

DELIGHT IN GOD

As parents, we also know how wonderful it feels when our children respond to our instruction with enthusiasm and obedience. We especially enjoy it when our children delight in our presence and appreciate us as their parents.

Notice how we then, naturally, want to respond in kind and share in their satisfaction when giving them what they wish. Likewise, it is easy to *Imagine God* wanting to respond in a generous way to us, as His children, when we delight in Him.

Psalm 37:4, NASB: *"Delight yourself in the LORD; And He will give you the desires of your heart."* Luke 11:13, NIV: *"If you then, though you are evil, know how to give good gifts to your children, how much more will your Father in heaven give the Holy Spirit to those who ask him!"*

LIVE FOR GOD'S KINGDOM

Consider your family once more. Isn't it natural to protect your spouse, your children, and yourself from predators and self-serving people whose intentions are not in your family's best interest?

Don't we desire true love, real friends and trustworthy people who contribute to our well-being and that of our loved ones? It is interesting that of all the people we have met in life, there is only a small number who we consider genuinely close.

Regardless of how many of us get there, God desires for us to be loving and trustworthy and, upon salvation, enter His kingdom. This is really good news as we *Imagine God* giving us this great opportunity for an eternal relationship with Him.

Matthew 7:14, NIV: *"But small is the gate and narrow the road that leads to life, and only a few find it."* Matthew 7:21, NIV: *"Not everyone who says to me, 'Lord, Lord,' will enter the kingdom of heaven, but only the one who does the will of my Father who is in heaven."* Psalm 145:20, NASB: *"The LORD keeps all who love Him, but all the wicked He will destroy."*

APPRECIATE GOD'S CREATIONS

Creativity is another characteristic with which we have all been blessed. Whether gardening, writing a poem, styling hair, building something or coloring pictures with our children, bringing a conceptual idea into reality is one of the most gratifying feelings that we can experience, especially when we are recognized for it. In fact, it can often feel euphoric!

Through these experiences, we are able to *Imagine God* in the way He enjoys creating things and the satisfaction He feels, especially when we recognize and appreciate Him for His creations.

With this in mind, recognizing that we are God's most precious creations, let's also appreciate ourselves and one another. We are His masterpieces worthy of respect and admiration.

Genesis 1:31, NIV: *"God saw all that he had made, and it was good."* Revelation 4:11, NIV: *"You are worthy, our Lord and God, to receive glory and honor and power, for you created all things, and by your will they were created and have their being."* Genesis 1:26, NIV: *"Then God said, 'Let us make mankind in our image, in our likeness, so that they may rule over the fish in the sea and the birds in the sky, over the livestock and all the wild animals, and over all the creatures that move along the ground.'"*

RETAIN GOD'S SPIRIT

As we mature, we learn to control our emotions and choose our reactions. We can discern which reactions are consistent with God's nature by tuning in to our feelings. Let's compare different feelings we experience and *Imagine God* by considering which of these are preferable: joy or anger, patience or impatience, kindness or rudeness, gratitude or discontent, forgiveness or resentment.

When I learned that the hired worker we discussed earlier had stolen from me, I became angry and resented being disregarded and victimized. Then I remembered that God is in control and looked at this as a test, a spiritual battle which I finally won by accepting it as a way to empathize and learn why we do not want to disregard God. Afterward, I was once again able to experience forgiveness, joy, and contentment.

1 John 4:8, NIV: *"Whoever does not love does not know God, because God is love."* 1 Corinthians 13:4–6, NIV: *"Love is patient, love is kind. . . . It is not easily angered, it keeps no record of wrongs. Love does not delight in evil but rejoices with the truth."* Galatians 5:22, NASB: *"But the fruit of the Spirit is love, joy, peace, patience, kindness, goodness, faithfulness."* Ephesians 6:12, KJB: *"For we wrestle not against flesh and blood, but against principalities, against powers, against the rulers of the darkness of this world, against spiritual wickedness in high places."*

FRIEND REQUEST GOD

In life, we regularly meet people and create new relationships—at work, church, school, in neighborhoods, and through social events. Now, consider how it feels to meet someone who is good-hearted: someone genuinely empathetic, who is a good listener and sincerely wishes you well. Isn't it natural to become less reserved with that person?

In truth, isn't this the type of person with whom you wish to share your time and build a meaningful relationship? It is easy to *Imagine God* wanting such a relationship as well. He naturally desires deeper, trusting, and fruitful relationships with us.

Matthew 5:8, NIV: *"Blessed are the pure in heart, for they will see God."* Jeremiah 17:10, NLT: *"But I, the LORD, search all hearts and examine secret motives. I give all people their due rewards, according to what their actions deserve."* Acts 13:22, KJB: *"He raised up unto them David to be their king; to whom also he gave testimony, and said, 'I have found David the son of Jesse, a man after mine own heart, which shall fulfil all my will.'"*

HUMBLE YOURSELF WITH GOD

Being spiritually mature, let us consider the nature of other individuals we tend to prefer and support: humble, meek, non-assuming individuals or people full of ego and arrogance? We have all met both types, in person and through the media.

Some celebrities, for example, may become prideful when earthly-focused people idolize them and treat them as if they are worthy of the adulation. Instead of becoming "puffed up," perhaps people should examine how God feels when we worship Him.

By reflecting on these preferences in our personal relationships, we can *Imagine God* wanting us to be humble as well.

2 Timothy 3:4–5, NLT: *"They will betray their friends, be restless, be puffed up with pride, and love pleasure rather than God. They will act religious, but they will reject the power that could make them godly. Stay away from people like that!"* Matthew 5:5, NLT: *"God blesses those who are humble, for they will inherit the whole earth."* James 4:10–12, KJB: *"Humble yourselves in the sight of the Lord, and he shall lift you up."* Micah 6:8, NLT: *"No, O people, the LORD has told you what is good, and this is what he requires of you: to do what is right, to love mercy, and to walk humbly with your God."* Numbers 12:3, NIV: *"Now Moses was a very humble man, more humble than anyone else on the face of the earth."*

BE A TRUE FRIEND TO ALL

Throughout our lives, we have experienced good times and bad times. Consider how many so-called friends were around when things were going well versus those bad times when you were lonely and really needed a friend.

In the same way that we learn who our true friends are when we are down, we can *Imagine God* is seeing the type of friend you and I are to those in need. Perhaps He is learning who His true friends will be during these times when His power and kingdom appear to be weak and elusive, relative to the power and prevalence we see from the devil. Maybe this is why God calls us to be kind to those less fortunate than ourselves.

Matthew 25:35–36, NIV: *"For I was hungry and you gave me something to eat, I was thirsty and you gave me something to drink, I was a stranger and you invited me in, I needed clothes and you clothed me, I was sick and you looked after me, I was in prison and you came to visit me."* Matthew 25:40, NIV: *"Truly I tell you, whatever you did for one of the least of these brothers and sisters of mine, you did for me."* Luke 14:13–14, NIV: *"But when you give a banquet, invite the poor, the crippled, the lame, the blind, and you will be blessed. Although they cannot repay you, you will be repaid at the resurrection of the righteous."*

ACKNOWLEDGE YOUR SIN

Reflect on a situation when you were mistreated by a remorseless person. Do you remember how you felt; how you may still feel? Now, visualize that person unexpectedly entering the room. Isn't it natural to wish they would leave so you wouldn't have to interact?

We can *Imagine God* as unable or unwilling to accept unrepentant sin, and having the same compulsion for separation when we have sinned against Him, until we acknowledge our wrongdoing and seek His forgiveness.

Maybe that is why Adam had to leave the Garden of Eden. First, he sinned, and then, rather than acknowledge his wrongdoing, he responded defensively when God confronted him (see Genesis 3:11-12).

Psalm 5:4, NASB: *"For You are not a God who takes pleasure in wickedness; No evil dwells with You."* 1 John 1:9, NLT: *"But if we confess our sins to him, he is faithful and just to forgive us our sins and to cleanse us from all wickedness."* Genesis 3:23, NASB: *"Therefore the LORD God sent him out from the garden of Eden, to cultivate the ground from which he was taken."* Isaiah 59:1–2, NASB: *"Behold, the LORD'S hand is not so short that it cannot save; nor is His ear so dull that it cannot hear. But your iniquities have made a separation between you and your God, and your sins have hidden His face from you so that He does not hear."* 1 Corinthians 15:22, NIV: *"For as in Adam all die, so in Christ all will be made alive."*

SEEK GOD'S FORGIVENESS

Negative feelings naturally result from being wronged. Animosity may develop and continue to build when the offender is unrepentant. This can tempt us to seek justice, perhaps wanting to inflict the same pain caused us, so they will come to feel remorseful and repent.

In the same way, we can *Imagine God* is a just God. Yet, most important, He is also a loving and forgiving God. Ultimately, He just wants us to repent of our sins and seek His forgiveness.

In judgment, will you prefer to be treated justly or with love and forgiveness? Will you choose punishment or salvation?

Leviticus 24:19, NASB *"If a man injures his neighbor, just as he has done, so it shall be done to him."* Ezekiel 18:32, NASB: *"'For I have no pleasure in the death of anyone who dies,' declares the Lord God. 'Therefore, repent and live.'"* Matthew 25:46, AKJV: *"And these shall go away into everlasting punishment: but the righteous into life eternal."*

FOLLOW GOD'S LEADERSHIP

The gift of being able to relate to God is intended to get to know Him so we can better serve Him, *not* to be Him. Sadly, prison is home to many people who have acted on their angry impulses by seeking revenge on those who have wronged them. They inappropriately took matters into their own hands, rather than leaving retribution to God. This is another example of how our sinful nature will take over when we disregard God and His leadership in our lives.

If you ever have a friend or loved one in a revengeful state of mind, wouldn't you advise that person to walk away from the situation because you realize that their vengeance will likely result in more harm to themselves than it is worth? Likewise, we can *Imagine God* is our confidant, aware of our short-sightedness and spiritual immaturity, the reason He cautions us not to act on revengeful thoughts.

Ephesians 4:26, KJB: *"Be ye angry and sin not: let not the sun go down upon your wrath."* Romans 12:19, NIV: *"Do not take revenge, my dear friends, but leave room for God's wrath, for it is written: 'It is mine to avenge; I will repay,' says the Lord."* 2 Thessalonians 1:6, NIV: *"God is just: He will pay back trouble to those who trouble you."*

FORGIVE OTHERS

Why is it important to forgive others? To begin with, true forgiveness will improve our state of health, physically, mentally, and spiritually. In the end, God will forgive us our sins.

How do we forgive? Recall an encounter when you were wronged. In the same way we are to confess our own sins, first acknowledge and accept that this incident did, in fact, occur. Next, really feel the painful emotions this brings. Then, force yourself to focus on anything positive that comes out of it: greater empathy for others; a deeper appreciation of what you have; maybe, a stronger trust in God, rather than people. It has been said that nothing happens *to* you, it happens *for* you to learn from. Be grateful for the lesson, and forgive!

Of all the ways that we can *Imagine God*, forgiveness is perhaps the most important, for this is the cornerstone of the new covenant. Maybe God intends for us to understand, appreciate, and re-create His love and forgiveness.

Romans 11:36, NLT: *"For everything comes from him and exists by his power and is intended for his glory. All glory to him forever! Amen."* Matthew 6:14, NIV: *"For if you forgive other people when they sin against you, your heavenly Father will also forgive you."* Matthew 6:12, NLT: *"And forgive us our sins, as we have forgiven those who sin against us."*

PART 3

PATH TO SALVATION

Now, consider a loved one with whom you have had a falling-out. Over a period of time, doesn't the pain caused from the offense fade and, as with God, you are left with a stronger desire to reunite and resume a loving relationship? Since God has existed much longer than we have, perhaps His desire for our love exceeds our comprehension. And, since scripture has convinced us of its truth, in part, by learning our true spiritual nature is like His and that we are, indeed, created in His own image, perhaps we should believe the most critical part of scripture regarding His gift of salvation, just as it was prophesied in the Old Testament (see Isaiah 53).

While we can identify with God as victim through the previous examples, we must also recognize that *we have played the part of offender too* one time or another, which is why *we need forgiveness*. In a leap of faith, we must acknowledge ourselves as sinners, then gain God's acceptance by dying unto ourselves and starting over as His—being *born again* spiritually through our Messiah, Jesus Christ.

* * *

1 Timothy 1:15, NIV: *"Christ Jesus came into the world to save sinners."*

Romans 6:23, NASB: *"For the wages of sin is death, but the free gift of God is eternal life in Christ Jesus our Lord."*

Romans 3:23, NIV: *"For all have sinned and fall short of the glory of God."*

John 8:24, NLT: *"That is why I said that you will die in your sins; for unless you believe that I Am who I claim to be, you will die in your sins."*

John 3:16, AKJV: *"For God so loved the world, that he gave his only begotten Son, that whoever believes in him should not perish, but have everlasting life."*

John 3:3, NIV: *"Jesus replied, 'Very truly I tell you, no one can see the kingdom of God unless they are born again.'"*

1 Corinthians 5:17–18, NASB: *"Therefore if anyone is in Christ, he is a new crea-*

ture; the old things passed away; behold, new things have come. Now all these things are from God, who reconciled us to Himself through Christ and gave us the ministry of reconciliation."

John 14:6, NIV: "Jesus answered, 'I am the way and the truth and the life. No one comes to the Father except through me.'"

John 20:29, NLT: "Then Jesus told him 'Blessed are those who believe without seeing me.'"

Hebrews 11:6, NLT: "And it is impossible to please God without faith. Anyone who wants to come to him must believe that God exists and that he rewards those who sincerely seek him."

John 8:34–36, NASB: "Jesus answered them, 'Truly, truly, I say to you, everyone who commits sin is the slave of sin. The slave does not remain in the house forever; the son does remain forever. So, if the Son makes you free, you will be free indeed.'"

John 10:10, NASB: "The thief comes only to steal and kill and destroy; I came that they may have life, and have it abundantly."

Matthew 5:24, NLT: *"Leave your sacrifice there at the altar. Go and be reconciled to that person. Then come and offer your sacrifice to God."*

NEXT STEP

The good news is that you can have an everlasting relationship with God and live in abundance as He intended—with love, joy, faith, and peace, rather than those unwanted feelings that plague us from our past experiences and decisions.

First, you must desire this relationship above all else. Second, recognize yourself as imperfect and, therefore, unfit to be received yet by God. Third, accept the greatest gift of all—the Messiah, Jesus Christ—with His blood and death on the cross paid the price for all of our iniquities. He will serve you in judgment by standing in your place before God. This important act of humility will also enable God to renew you and bring about purpose for your life.

To accept His free gift, simply embrace what is written in Romans 10:9, NASB: *"that if you confess with your mouth Jesus as Lord, and* believe in your heart that God raised Him from the dead, you will be saved!"

To experience transformation, demonstrate your conviction. Forgive and accept your own self by truly accepting Jesus as the bearer of your sins. Now you can let go of guilt, shame, and regret. Instead, *believe, be grateful, and become renewed.*

Matthew 9:5, NIV: *"Which is easier: to say, 'Your sins are forgiven,' or to say, 'Get up and walk'?"*

Matthew 6:33, NIV: *"But seek first his king-dom and his righteousness, and all these things will be given to you as well."*

Philippians 4:7, AKJV: *"And the peace of God, which passes all understanding, shall keep your hearts and minds through Christ Jesus."*

Psalm 25:18, AKJV: *"Look on my affliction and my pain; and forgive all my sins."*

Colossians 1:14, KJB: *"In whom we have redemption through his blood, even the forgiveness of sins."*

Psalm 32:1, AKJV: *"Blessed is he whose transgression is forgiven, whose sin is covered."*

Philipians 4:13, NLT: *"For I can do everything through Christ, who gives me strength."*

PART 4

AUTHOR'S TESTIMONY

Not long after graduating from the University of Florida, I began an export distribution business and felt that I was on my way to becoming a successful businessman. I frequently traveled through the Caribbean, and it was there on the island of Trinidad where I met my wife, Joyce. We have now been married for more than twenty years.

After selling packaging equipment and materials with marginal success, I left that business to pursue my newfound passion for real estate, certain that when I made a lot of money, everything would be great and I would never feel insecure again.

My first real estate project failed miserably. Instead of amassing a fortune, I found myself starting over. I lost my money, confidence, self-esteem, and hope. I was broken! Back then, I was convinced that religion and talk of God were only for people who needed a crutch because they were never successful.

After much searching, desperate for new hope, and by listening to other people's testimony, as well as identifying with scripture, I finally determined that my *real* discomfort was due to being separated from God. I then became aware of *only one way* to break that separation and proceeded to ask Jesus into my life. Being raised Jewish, this was taboo, the opposite of everything that I had ever been taught. Now, with help from my wife, I am learning that life is less about me and more about God.

After eighteen years, I continue to travel this road and enjoy a relationship with God. Along the way, I have learned what it means to be created "in His own image" and the value it offers us.

On July 22, 2015, I suffered a massive heart attack and, subsequently, underwent quadruple bypass surgery. Surprisingly, I survived that experience feeling much better than I had felt in decades. It was during my recovery that I decided to write this book. After all, I never heard this message preached, and I knew that it could be meaningful to others as well. I think this is part of God's purpose for my life.

I believe that God had already saved me spiritually and now, physically, as well. Presently, I try and live my life in service to Him.

At the time of my heart attack, I was surprised to learn that all of my coronary arteries were severely occluded and death was near. Similarly, whether we realize it or not, we are all spiritually in need of God to perform heart surgery through Jesus, and only after it has been performed can we then clearly feel the difference.

PHOTO OF THE RISING SUN

©2016 Richard Scott Pribell

Author Rick Pribell read the following prophesy from Zechariah on the night of December 16th, 2014:

"...because of the tender mercy of our God,
by which the rising sun will
come to us from heaven
to shine on those living in darkness
and in the shadow of death,
to guide our feet into the path of peace."
Luke 1:78-79, NIV

The very next morning Rick woke up to this glorious sunrise as seen on the front cover, and photographed it from the balcony of his hotel room in Melbourne Beach, Florida. This actually was a "rising sun" that "came to [him]...to shine...in darkness," an image of a "path", "to guide [his] feet".

A few weeks later, he heard the following message at church regarding the baptism of Jesus, which occurred 30 years after Zechariah's prophesy:

"In those days Jesus came from Nazareth
of Galilee and was baptized by John
in the Jordan. And just as he was
coming up out of the water, he saw
the heavens torn apart and the Spirit
descending like a dove on him..."
Mark 1:9-11

What was witnessed at His baptism may also be interpreted in this photograph. The light, for example, appears to be "torn open". Moreover, the image can be seen as a "dove" as though it is "descending". To see it, visualize the clouds as wings, the sun as the head, and the remaining light as its body and tail. Rick found it extraordinary how both of those scripture verses describe, in detail, this very sunrise.

Over time, an abstract outline of the crucifix appeared to him which can be seen by superimposing a cross behind the image, as depicted on the back cover. Notice its precise dimensions and reflection of light at the base. The dove can be perceived as Jesus with the tail, elevated, as His feet flared outward.

Could this be a re-creation of the sunrise that was both prophesied by Zechariah and witnessed at the baptism of Jesus? If so, maybe God was delivering to us this image as a sign for what was about to come; His loving response to the sacrifice of His Son, who asked that we be forgiven while dying on the cross for our sins. The experience initiated a new beginning for Rick, calling him to share his relationship with God, and to help others discover God for themselves.

Through baptism, we share in a symbolic way the experience of Jesus. As we descend beneath the water, we remember that Jesus died for our sins; and as we emerge into the light, we commemorate with joy that He was raised to everlasting life. Look again at the photograph, and perhaps you too will see His image on the cross as you *Imagine God* in your life.

CPSIA information can be obtained
at www.ICGtesting.com
Printed in the USA
FFHW010525240719
53815811-59507FF